HOLD ME TIGHT

also by
Jason Schneiderman

Sublimation Point (2004)
Striking Surface (2010)
Primary Source (2016)
Queer: A Reader for Writers (2016)

HOLD ME TIGHT

POEMS

JASON SCHNEIDERMAN

 Red Hen Press | *Pasadena, CA*

Book layout by Wesley Griffith and Sandra Moore
Painting of author by Don Bachardy, courtesy of the artist

Library of Congress Cataloging-in-Publication Data

Names: Schneiderman, Jason, author.
Title: Hold me tight : poems / Jason Schneiderman.
Description: First Edition. | Pasadena, CA : Red Hen Press, [2020]
Identifiers: LCCN 2019055299 | ISBN 9781597098298 (trade paperback) | ISBN
   9781597098304 (ebook)
Subjects: LCGFT: Poetry.
Classification: LCC PS3619.C4473 H65 2020 | DDC 811/.6—dc23
LC record available at https://lccn.loc.gov/2019055299

The National Endowment for the Arts, the Los Angeles County Arts Commission, the Ahmanson Foundation, the Dwight Stuart Youth Fund, the Max Factor Family Foundation, the Pasadena Tournament of Roses Foundation, the Pasadena Arts & Culture Commission and the City of Pasadena Cultural Affairs Division, the City of Los Angeles Department of Cultural Affairs, the Audrey & Sydney Irmas Charitable Foundation, the Kinder Morgan Foundation, the Meta & George Rosenberg Foundation, the Allergan Foundation, the Riordan Foundation, Amazon Literary Partnership, and the Mara W. Breech Foundation partially support Red Hen Press.

First Edition
Published by Red Hen Press
www.redhen.org

Acknowledgments

Grateful acknowledgement is made to the editors of the following publications, where many of these poems initially appeared, often in slightly different forms.

The *Academy of American Poets* Poem-a-Day, "sugar is smoking"; the *American Poetry Review*, "Peter and the Wolf Orchestra," "Scorpion and Wolf," "Wolf," "Wolf and Fox," "Wolves and Sleep"; *Bellevue Literary Review*, "In Memoriam, Fanny Imlay (1794-1816)"; *Best American Poetry 2018*, "Voxel"; *Columbia Journal*, "Storyteller"; the *Cortland Review*, "Writing About _____ in the Age of Google"; *Dark Ink: A Poetry Anthology Inspired by Horror*, "*Little Red Riding Hood*, Season 12"; *How Did This Happen?: Poems for the Not So Young Anymore*, "sugar is smoking"; the *Literary Review*, "Americana," "Voxel"; *Plume*, "The Last Mirror," "The Last Widow"; *Poems in the Aftermath*, "Anger"; the *Poetry Review*, "The Last Abortion," "The Last Baby," "The Last Black Hole," "The Last Book," "The Last Typist"; *Resist Much, Obey Little*, "The Last Form," "Rapture"; and *Still Life with Poem*, selections from "The Chris Burden Suite."

Contents

I.

IV.

V. The Book of Lasts

I.

Anger

When I was angry,
I kept asking how
anger works.
No one understood

my question.
Friends thought I was joking.
Or being obtuse.
Friends would say: What

do you mean
how anger works.
Anger is anger. What
are you asking.

And I would say:
Well. Is anger
a finite
material.

Is anger like hydrogen,
and there's simply
a certain amount
of it in the universe.

Is there a zero sum
of anger, a law
of the conservation
of anger,

and can we
pass it back
and forth.

Can you take my anger
and leave me less?
Can I take your anger
and then have more?

Is anger a renewable
resource, like trees
or coral reef, subject
to natural rhythms

and mass die offs,
forest fires,
and warming tides,
cycles of growth and depletion.

Is anger something
you deplete like money,
that you save or spend
and is gone as it goes,

or something replenished
like ejaculate,
more on the way
as soon as you send some off,

or is anger like ova,
each egg coming
on its own schedule,
until they run out.

Is anger like pus,
a response to a wound,
that you can drain,
or that you can heal,

or is anger like a gas
you can vent
because it is compressible
but combustible,

or is anger like water
that will explode
the water balloon
unless you tie it off

at the right time.
I thought someone
had to know
the answer

because I was consumed
by anger,
it was under
everything I did

I felt it all the time,
all the time,
and it never
departed.

I didn't have a breakdown,
though I asked friends
if what I was experiencing
was a breakdown (no,

they said, a breakdown
looks only
like a breakdown), and
I looked OK,

but no one knew
how to help me,
and I told a friend
that I wasn't OK

and she told me
that I was OK,
but the anger was there
all the time,

like a pair of shoes
that were always
between me
and the ground I walked on,

and I kept asking everyone
how anger works:
Can you drain it?
Can you vent it?

Can you stop it?
Can you heal it?
Can you trade it?
Can you sell it?

And no one,
no one, no one,
no one knew
what I was asking

until finally
someone asked me
to describe
what I was feeling,

and she said
you're not talking
about anger,
you're talking about rage,

and I realized
that I've never
experienced anger.
I've only known rage.

Which helped a lot.
Which explained why
I could only think
about striking out

and then not strike out.
Which explained why
I knew which plants
in my garden could be made

into poisons, and how.
Which explained
why my daydreams
turned into

elaborate fantasies
about harming people,
until I did the things
I imagined to myself,

and listen, please listen,
I knew it was bad,
and I wanted out, but
I couldn't write

my way out of it,
and I couldn't think
my way out of it,
and I couldn't love

my way out of it,
and I couldn't read
my way out of it,
and I thought I would live

with it forever,
that I would contain
it at whatever price
I had to pay,

and I'm telling you this,
and I need you to listen,
because I'm saying
that I do understand

what it's like to want
everyone else to suffer
as much as you
are suffering,

and I understand
what it's like
to want to die
both to contain

the pain of rage,
and to spread
the pain of rage,
and when you read

of this mass murder or
that suicide bombing, know,
these killers are not
inhuman or monstrous,

but rather that they are
weak vessels for rage,
that they are balloons
that have burst with their rage,

that they are pipe bombs made
of flesh and bone,
and peace is what I want
more than anything else,

but peace is so fragile,
so easy to take, so easy
to lose, and so they take it
from you, to feel less alone,

and I'm out of it now
because I thought
I had done it to myself,
but I didn't. I see

that now. I'm closer
to peace. I'm further
from rage. I'm a bomb
no longer ticking,

but I was a bomb.
Hold me tight.
I was a bomb.
Hold me tight.

II. The Book of Wolves

Scorpion and Wolf

"Shouldn't you be Frog?" Scorpion asks.
"Every time I do this story, it's with Frog."

Wolf laughs. "Are you scared? You always
drown anyway. What do you care?"

Scorpion starts to cry. "We can't be
in this story together. The water is rising,

and Frog is supposed to be here. I know
how the story goes." Wolf shrugs.

"Stay here and drown," Wolf says. "Your
stinger is nothing to my tough hide."

Scorpion refuses to climb on Wolf's back,
and the water keeps rising, as he hops around.

"You had a chance to survive the story,"
Wolf says. "Looks like you blew it."

Peter and the Wolf Orchestra

After the conductor refuses to listen
to their demands, the wolf members
of the orchestra simply refuse to play
during the season's first performance
of *Peter and the Wolf.* The conductor
pushes forward, and audience members
are unsure of how to show solidarity
with the silent wolf players. The wolves
are fired, and re-form as the first
all-wolf orchestra, and choose *Peter
and the Wolf* as their first production,
though for the first time, Peter is cast
as the villain, and the wolf as the hero.
Many parents complain, as children
who attend the performance are deeply
ashamed of being Peters, and often
spend their days insisting that they
want to be wolves, and some even
try to run away from home to join
the wolves. Very few of the children
succeed in becoming wolves, though
some of them do. Some people say
you can tell a wolf who used to be
a human child. Some people say you
can't.

Parable of the Wolves (ii)

Wolf loves Fox, which wolves don't do.
Wolf loves Fox, which makes all the other
wolves hate him. All the wolves are named Wolf,
which usually works fine, but now that Wolf
loves Fox, they need a name to drive him
from them. They call him Foxlovingwolf,
and the wolves drive him from the forest
with Fox, and Fox and Foxlovingwolf live
in a field, which suits Fox just fine. At the end
of their lives, Fox reveals that he was really a wolf.
Foxlovingwolf starts to cry, and says "Why
would you do that to me? I gave up everything
for you and I didn't have to?" Foxbutreallywolf says
"It was the only way I could be sure of you.
I had to know you would give everything up
for me."

Storyteller

for RZ

Little Red Riding Hood is the most told story
in the world. There are so many versions
that at the School for Storytellers, one student
is picked to learn nothing but versions of *Little
Red Riding Hood.* Do you see that girl in the corner?
The one crying? She's just been told that she will never learn
any other story. She's going to try to escape, to go join her sisters
at the shoe factory, but no one escapes the School for Storytellers.
She's going to become the most famous storyteller of all time.
She's going to fill auditoriums and amphitheaters and football stadiums
because everyone loves the story of *Little Red Riding Hood.*
Everyone loves to hear it over and over again, and she tells it infinitely,
with variety and power and charm. When she dies, the obituaries
will be critical of her for having sent every one of her children to work
at the shoe factory with their aunts and cousins, where they stand on the line
cursing their mother for hours each day, but as soon as they're on break,
and as soon as they get home, they read any story they damn well please.

Parable of the Wolves (i)

My mother married a wolf, but everyone insisted
that he wasn't a wolf. Everyone felt sorry for him
because he had been raised by wolves, and often
my mother would tell me how lucky I was not to be
raised by a wolf, even though I was being raised
by a wolf. When my mother died, my wolf father
married another wolf. They asked me why I wasn't
a wolf. I said, "I thought you weren't wolves,"
and as they tore into my flesh, they said "Of course
we're wolves, you stupid sheep."

Little Red Riding Hood, Season 12

You'd think people would get tired of it
by now, the way the Wolf dies at the end
of every season, but turns out not to have
died, and certainly, fans point out that the
Joker never dies in the *Batman* comics,
that Blofeld is always on his way back to
battle James Bond, and if anything,
the complaint that gains the most traction
is not that the Wolf should meet a singular
fate, like Circe or Moriarty (even though
he had his own tendency to come back),
but rather at how much more extreme
the peril that Little Red is placed in
each season. In Season 8, the use of medieval
torture devices was extremely upsetting.
Several parenting organizations
boycotted the show after the suggestion
that Little Red had been experiencing
flashbacks in Season 10, and that there
had been no Wolf at all, only her fears and
trauma. I found Season 11 the hardest
to take, and more or less stopped watching
after Little Red was doused in gasoline
and sobbed while the Wolf flicked lit matches
at her and the two corrupt cops in league
with the Wolf explained to her how
they would cover it up. The bathtub scene
in Season 12 didn't entirely surprise me,
but still, that happened to someone

I know, and I won't be watching Season 13,
when they've promised to finally
kill the Wolf and fill him full of stones,
because even if they keep their promise
there'll be another season as long as
there are still viewers. That's how stories
work, how they keep getting told,
over and over and over,
as long as people will listen.

Wolves and Sleep

Wolves do not suffer insomnia, which is generally
believed to have been caused by a lack of fear
in early wolves. People, on the other hand, do suffer
insomnia, owing to an abundance of fear
in early humans. Insomnia is believed to have its origins
in that first man by the fire, trying to stay awake,
to keep the fire going, to keep the wolves at bay.
Insomnia is believed to have begun with that first
woman, unable to see in the dark, lighting a lamp
or inventing a candle to illuminate the predatory
darkness. "We can see day or night," say the wolves.
"We can hunt day or night," say the wolves. "You hunt us,"
say the humans. "Your hunt is our insomnia."

Little Red Riding Wolf

On the lecture circuit, Little Red Riding Wolf
is generally brought to tears by at least one
question. Wolves tend to accuse her of being
a collaborator, while humans tend to demand
to know if she has ever eaten a person herself.

Folklorists tend to dismiss her outright
as being trapped in a very stupid story,
while a certain cadre of literary theorists
consider her very identity an ouroboros,
a figure that they hope will become as popular

as the rhizome once became for an earlier
generation of scholars. None of this helps
Little Red Riding Wolf, whose only real
pleasure is cruising online dating apps,
never meeting up, but pretending

sometimes to be only a wolf,
sometimes to be only a little girl.

Parable of the Wolves (iii)

Wolves are overrepresented in academia,
despite their relatively small numbers
in the general population, having been
nearly hunted to extinction. They often
meet with bears and snakes to discuss
how badly they are portrayed in various
media. They often eat their students.

III. The Chris Burden Suite

The Chris Burden Suite

In Memoriam, Chris Burden 1946–2015.

1. "Velvet Water" (1974)

Watching a man
trying to "breathe water"
is a lot like watching a man
trying to drown himself.

At first, you want to stop him,
to take his head out of the bucket,
to insist that it's a lovely idea,
but no one can actually breathe

water, and then you worry
for him, and then you worry
less for him, and then
you wish he'd stop.

At first it's awful,
like a horror movie
where the things are
really happening,

and then it's tedious,
since he won't drown, and he
won't stop trying to drown,
excuse me—breathe water—

and the suffering
is there for you
to witness
as "art."

Or not.
You can go.
As he reminded
you at the start of the reel,

this is a recording. It's not happening.
It's not even what happened.
It's just a record, just a way
of thinking yourself back.

2.

How long did they stand on the ladders?

    All night.

And the water was electrified?

    Yes. With live wires. Cables, really.

What would have happened if they had stepped in the water?

    Death? Pain?

You don't know very much about the effects of electric current on the human body, do you?

    Not really.

But you're afraid of them?

    Yes.

Very afraid?

    Yes.

Would that be a good enough reason to stand on a ladder above the thing you fear, and face it down?

For me?

Yes.

No.

3. A brief essay outlining my objections to movements that attempt to collapse (or by collapsing, discover) the boundaries between life and art.

First of all, art is already a part of one's life, assuming that it is somewhere in your experience at all. I may not see the moon all day long, but that does not mean that I am somehow quarantining or isolating the moon from my daytime exploits and treating Earth's only natural satellite as something that has no place until someone "collapses" the boundaries between day and night. When I am in a museum it is because I have gone to a museum. I am still in my life, and that is OK with me. I like my life. It is a very nice life, and in my life, I see very nice art.

Secondly, I highly object to the commodification of my life by artists who claim to collapse a boundary that I, personally, do not find problematic. My silence is my silence, not a musical piece. My observation of a cloud is my observation of a cloud, and simply put, if I draw a line and then erase it, that is not your art work, it is my experience. If I am an artist, it may be my art, but it is only ever the willful enaction of art that creates art. My slumbering while you film me is not acting, though the result may be art.

Thirdly: As of yet, no art or artist has been able to "collapse" this boundary without creating a new boundary. For example, even if the wall text invites you to "complete the art" in some certain way, you will be thrown out of the gallery if you actually express an artistic impulse of your own. The performance artists may be nude, but do not try to strip down yourself and join in, or again, security will be called. Certainly all artists want their art to be experienced as part of the life of their audience, and there is a magical friction when the art enters the life of the viewer, but efforts to break down that magical space as though it were an obstruction is precisely what led Chris Burden to silently ask himself during his piece "Doomed": "[M]y God, don't they care anything at all about me? Are they going to leave me here to die?"

4.

If I got on an elevator,
and I were told to stick
push-pins in the artist,

I think I'd say no.

5.

I hope I'd say no.

6. "All the Submarines of the United States of America," 1987

The submarines are undeniably beautiful,
suspended from the ceiling in a field
that makes one want to live underwater,
and that's the problem, right? The cuteness,
the way that the adorable becomes the
loveable when you were supposed
to reject the whole system. You shouldn't
say "What beautiful submarines!" You should say
"Oh God, look at all that destruction we've
unleashed on the world!" But really,
those are some beautiful submarines.

7. "All the Submarines of the United States of America," 1987

A submarine is a submarine is a submarine.

Something there is that doesn't love a submarine.

Thirteen ways of looking at a submarine.

You do not submarine, you do not submarine.

In the middle of my life, a submarine.

Because I could not stop for submarine.

Without even trying, I can think of a half dozen submarine.

So much depends upon a submarine.

The art of submarine isn't hard to master.

And everything was submarine, submarine, submarine.

8. "Shoot," 1971

The fame began with the photograph,
the earnest boy with a bandaged arm,
black and white, facing the camera
guileless, the wound a kind of anti-pose,
a kind of pornography, a kind of insistence
that what you see is real, because it is true
he was shot, on purpose, by his own design,
for art. What do you love enough
to be shot for? What do you believe in
enough to be shot for?

Nothing?

Me neither.

IV.

Rapture

There's a movie about a woman who can't love God.
It's a terrible movie. Low budget. Poorly acted.
It's clumsy and obvious, but I used to watch it over and over
because it had something I needed: a woman, who,
visited by God, cannot love him. Her husband is dead,
her daughter too, both murdered, not senselessly,
but by a man they had tried to help, a man who took
revenge for something that was his own fault. Life,
in the movie, is a test. Life is a test, that in her suffering,
she has passed, except that in having suffered, she has also
failed, because now, she cannot love God, and she is refused,
by her own honesty, from the Kingdom of Heaven.
What the movie says is that life is not a test.
What the movie says is that even if life is designed
to be a test, we cannot help but love our lives so much
that they are everything, and we are right to love our lives
in such a way that we could even refuse heaven,
if it meant giving up on what we have here. It has been
years since I watched that movie, and I think perhaps
it's because now, at the end of every day, I lie down
next to you, and that as long as your arm holds me firm
as I enter the country of sleep, I will never have to choose
between you and heaven. And if I did have to choose,
I might choose nothing, like that woman forever
in purgatory, because in the middle of my life, I could not
love a God who would let these things happen. I needed
that story once; I'm telling it to you now,
because I know I may need it again.

Voxel

O newest of new words,
welcome to my mouth!

Though you are still not
in the dictionary (yet),

you are transparent in meaning:
a pixel with volume,

the basic unit of 3-D
printing, and now that we have

you, voxel, Plato will have
to let us back in his Republic

because we can print beds
and guns and pots and pans,

and for so long, we thought
that nothing could be imagined

until it was imagined by us;
and if now, like those monks

in that story, where they
end the world by finding

every possible arrangement
for the letters in the name

of God, we too can see
everything that can ever

be photographed
or represented visually,

at least to the sighted,
then pixels mean

that we can predict
everything that might

ever be seen by creating
an algorithm to generate

every permutation of every
image that could ever

be arranged out of pixels
and yes, the permutations

are so many as to be infinite
for all practical purposes

because we die, because
we can more easily calculate

the number of possibilities
than actually look at them,

and yes, this was always
in our eyes, because pixels

are merely externalized
rods and cones

but still, every single one
of those possibilities is there

in that algorithm, or in the
idea of that algorithm,

and you, little voxel,
are still a primitive thing,

a gradation so coarse as to
evoke Donkey Kong in

its earliest days
of blocky charm,

but refinement
is our human skill,

so much more so
than love or penmanship

or peacemaking, at which
we have learned little, but now,

voxel, everything is contained
inside you—not fire

perhaps—but our model
of fire—not affection,

perhaps—but our model
of affection, and dear voxel,

the smaller you become,
the more powerful you will be.

Dear voxel, already
I am beginning to think

of myself in terms of you,
and sweet voxel, the day

is coming when I will print
my selfies as tiny dioramas

made of you, and you will know
that you contain all

that is human
in the universe,

that you hold everything
in versatile potential,

my neurons, my face,
my planet, my stem cells,

my lover, my spaceship,
my coffin, my poems,

my eyesight, my corpse.

OK, Earth.

I'll learn to love rot.

I'll learn to love things

that are rotting. I'll learn

to see that in many kinds

of death there are also

kinds of life, and I'll learn

to see that life and death

are interdependent.

I'll learn to compost,

and I'll learn to love

composting. I'll learn

to love fertility, although

it is something I will never

achieve, until I myself

am fertilizer. I get it,

Earth. I was never as sterile

as I thought. I saw myself

as one thing, but I was

another. I was looking out

from my body, so I couldn't

really see my body. But still,

Earth, is it OK if I keep

loving sterility too?

Is it all right if I still love

clean white surfaces?

Marble. Porcelain.

I can't unlove bleached linens,

or a black leather couch,

wiped down. I'll still love

Glass. Clear glass.

And a man's sperm,

dying on my chest,

or in my mouth.

I'm going to love that too.

At the core of a nuclear

reactor, under the water,

it glows blue. It's almost

the same blue as the wall

of a glacier, when cleared

of snow, and polished,

but in the reactor it gives

off its own light,

like an appliance

in my kitchen, in the dark.

It's a sun, underwater,

but blue and deadly

and quarantined,

safe in all respects

except the waste,

the forever lasting waste.

in black capsules,

the opposite of life,

the end of the glow,

anti-fecundity in a color,

the opposite of life,

remainder of what warms you,

or cools you, if it's summer.

I don't want to love

that blue anymore.

I want to love the soil,

and the worms.

My best chance

at giving life

to another thing.

My best chance

to survive.

Americana

You're all hat and no cattle.

You're all snake and no venom.

You're all wood and no lead.

You're all tar and no feather.

You're all ranger and no power.

You're all margin and no center.

You're all show and no dog.

You're all speedo and no dick.

You're all barricade and no protest.

You're all outbreak and no virus.

You're all New York and no city.

You're all box and no Cornell.

You're all inch and no foot.

You're all ruler and no measure.

Writing About _____ in The Age of Google

The firework he rested on his head
killed him instantly when he set it off.

It happened in Maine, in _____.
It was all over the news, and time was,

I would have written about it,
used his name without thinking twice,

quoted the news source, shown
everything. I might have made him

a symbol for something larger,
or imagined his thoughts, made up

a few details, but not now,
when I suspect that the people

who loved him are likely to Google him,
to find what I write. Perhaps this should

always have been the case, that what
I was about to do was to instrumentalize

him, to make his death serve my work.
Perhaps it would have been a good poem.

Perhaps not. Perhaps it would have moved
you, reader. Perhaps not. But now,

it will never exist, to spare
the people who loved him

the chance of stumbling across
my little poem of interpretation,

which I might have titled,
"What _____'s Death Means to Me,"

when the truth is that it means nothing
to me, while to those who loved him,

his life was the center of a universe,
the way every life is the center

of someone's universe, and every life
deserves to be mourned,

even the lives ended in ways so foolish
as to be, to the unacquainted, laughable.

In Memoriam, Fanny Imlay (1794–1816)

When you ask yourself how people survived
the nineteenth century, before soap and
antibiotics, before anesthesia and electricity,
remember that not all of them did.
Remember Fanny Imlay in her
hotel room, drafting her suicide note
before drinking laudanum. Remember
the inn keeper, who found her corpse,
and tore her name from the bottom
of the note so that she could be buried
in Christian ground. Remember Fanny Imlay's
final words, offering *the blessing of forgetting*
that such a creature ever existed, as I
[remainder torn away]

sugar is smoking

it's amazing how death
is always around the corner,
or not even so far away
as that, hiding in the little pleasures
that some of us would go
so far as to say
are the only things
keeping us alive

V. The Book of Lasts

The Last Book

The last book tries to remember
the last time someone read it;
tries to remember if someone
has ever read it all. The last book
isn't sure what it's about, because
it can't open its own pages, the
way you can't open your own chest,
and you've never seen your
own organs. The last book
has no other books to ask about
what it feels like to be read
because that's what it means
to be the last, and the last book
doesn't even know that it's just
zeros and ones, hurtling through
space, sent into the universe
by people who died millennia
ago on a planet that's long since
been eaten by the sun it revolved
around. The last book still
thinks it's paper and ink,
bookboard and cloth,
and if anyone ever picks up
the signal, maybe it will be again.

The Last Widow

The last widow misses men. The last widow misses her husband
a great deal, but she also liked men in general. She refuses
all of the invitations to appear on the morning news shows until
the medical bills turn out to be more than she can swing, and she
accepts the money to be interviewed. The last widow tries, this time
on air, to explain that the past wasn't like what people think it was,
and how now that the only thing anyone knows of men are from
Victorian novels and internet pornography, people have a skewed
idea of what men were like, and no, she's not saying that rape wasn't
a problem, and yes, we do have more options with the wonderful
things that are being done with silicone, but really, it wasn't just
penises that she liked, and in fact her own husband's wasn't at all like
the ones you see in the surviving documents, and really, no woman
she knew behaved like the women in those videos, so can't you
understand that most of the men were different too? Some of her
friends suggest that she seek comfort with one of the young people
who have the facial hair that's so in style now, and the last widow
wants to say, "I'm not a lesbian," but that word doesn't have much
meaning now, in a world without men, and it's not really that she
wants a substitute for the husband she misses, as much as that she wishes
people understood what it is that she wants back.

The Last Mirror

The last mirror was put on trial. The last mirror was accused
of inciting vanity, of lacking originality, of encouraging vice,
of being nothing more than a parrot or an echo.

The last mirror's defense was that Echo had shown devotion
to the man she loved, and that parrots love their pirates.
The last mirror insisted that vanity, like greed, can be good,

because really, every man should love himself. The last mirror
argued that vice is a lot of fun every now and then,
and that imitation can also be a form of love,

why even Freud, that old master, could not distinguish between
the desire to possess and the desire to be. The last mirror
lost the case. As you may have guessed, it was a show trial.

The judge said that love is not a defense, and even ejected
the viewer who laughed when the prosecutor
asked the mirror in a froth of rage and anger

"What's love got to do with it?" entirely unaware of the song
by the same name. The judge ordered the last mirror
shattered into a hundred thousand pieces on the courtroom floor.

When the bailiff had shattered the last mirror,
each one of the pieces proclaimed that now
it was the last mirror, however small the piece might have been.

The judge held the prisoners
in contempt
and called every piece a liar.

The Last Baby

The last baby is only the last baby for a year or so.
then he's the last toddler, then the last teenager,
then the last person. He makes lists of things
to pass the time, lists with entries like, "I am the last
speaker of any human language" and "I am the last
masturbator of all time" and "I am the last graffiti artist."
He writes on the walls because no one can stop him,
and he makes a list of all the things that make him feel
less alone, like episodes of *The Twilight Zone* and pillows
that are shaped like people. "I was the last baby," he writes
in chalk in a parking lot by the 7-11, hoping that when the rain
washes it away, it will cease to be true. "I was the last
toddler" he writes inside the front cover of a leather bound
edition of William Shakespeare's *Compleat Works*
and "I was the last person who knew how to read this"
on a street sign showing the entrance to the Holland
Tunnel. One day he makes his last list. He calls it
"The last list."

The Last Form

"What you are describing," my teacher said,
"is a circle, and as they do not exist in the material realm,
it is not merely foolish to think of one, but actually
unethical." He explained to the class how for tragic
millennia there were terrible time-wasters known
as philosophers and how they tried to convince
everyone that there were things in the world
that were not in the world. Of course, they had long since
been put to death, and while we kept their memory alive
merely to avoid their mistakes, we should never forget
at what cost we might make those mistakes as well. This
was almost sixty years ago. I am an old man now, and I have
fathered children, and I have worked a very long time, and
I have retired, and now I tell stories to my grandchildren
and I know that I am forgetting more and more. I tell myself
the story of that day as a ritual, to remember who I am,
and to fight the fog that comes. This is the one thing
I have never told anyone. I still believe in the circle.
I may be the last, but I believe.

The Last Abortion

The Last Abortion wins the Pulitzer Prize
for Columbia Historian Carrie Selma,
the bestselling book reminding the nation
of the mostly forgotten story of how completely
divided the United States had once been over
a somewhat gruesome biological process
rendered mercifully obsolete by the "marsupial procedure"
over one hundred years ago. Selma thrills
her audience with slides from the twentieth
century battles, angry faces next to octagonal
and circular signs, though she leaves the really gory
images for an inset in the book for the truly macabre
or brave. In her lectures, she mentions
the antiquated phrase "the birth canal" in passing,
knowing that this will be the focus
of every Q&A, her audience shocked
by the idea of babies as little gondolas
forcing their way out of the Venice
of their mothers.

The Last Typist

The last typist is an act in the carnival. Parents show their children
how writing used to be done, after pens, but before the computers
just did what you say. In one part of the act, the last typist competes
with a computer to type up sentences that even the best voice
recognition software can't quite get right. Sentences like "Tulah's
two tulle tu-tus took two tons of tulle" in the all ages show, and then
naughty sentences like, "Mike Hunt is so poorly behaved, I spend
hours spanking Mike Hunt" in the show just for grownups. The last typist
types ninety words a minutes, which she knows wasn't much in the time
of typists, but as that time has passed, she'll settle for her gifts
such as they are.

The Last Ace of Base Enthusiast

The last Ace of Base Enthusiast wishes she could live in the 1990s.
The last Ace of Base Enthusiast imagines a world where it was impossible
to avoid Ace of Base—where it would be playing over the stereo
when you entered a convenience store, or when you went to the bank.
At first she was annoyed when her friends asked her what the songs meant,
or tried to pin her down on precisely what "the sign" was, or insisted
on knowing why the main character was crying in "Don't Turn Around."
Later, she was frustrated when her friends refused to listen to her answers,
and she had to write a book explaining all of the lyrics, and the multiple
permutations by which they might be understood. No one bought the book,
so she started making dioramas of the convenience stores and banks
in the 1990s where you couldn't avoid Ace of Base songs. Her show
of dioramas is well received, and highly regarded as an example of
"The New Retrospectivists" though she is consistently hurt by the pride that
critics take in being able "to endure the hideous cacophony of screeching
vocals that the artist has dredged up from a past that we remember with
great pain, but as she has shown us, forget at our own peril." Once, she thinks,
people would have bought the CD in the gift shop on the way out of the museum,
back in the 1990s, when there were CDs.

The Last War

The project was simple, though initially most people
regarded it as misguided. We removed everyone under
the age of twelve from every armed conflict. Anyone
from twelve to eighteen could stay and fight, or go.
Up to them. Adults left in war zones were sterilized,
using a gas cloud that could be wafted over battlefields,
starving the conflicts of new combatants. Many people
were sure that the children, raised abroad by strangers,
would continue the conflicts, but having anticipated
that probability, plans were carefully developed. The adoptive
parents were instructed to give contradictory answers,
saying things like, "Oh, wait, no . . . your parents were
Sunni, not Shiia . . . or maybe Sufi . . ." or "No, I'm fairly
sure you were Irish, or was it English?" If the children
demanded proof, our office created specially forged family
trees, to show one Hutu and one Tutsi parent, or one
Conquistador and one Aztec parent, or one Nazi and one
Jew. It took a long time—generations—and our critics
likened it to genocide or ethnic cleansing, and in a way
it was, but every person on the planet watched the last war
with great pity, the last two survivors of some ancient conflict,
the war zones having gotten smaller and smaller, easily
monitored with drones and satellite imaging. The last
combatant shot the second to last combatant and he
rejoiced to have won, to have claimed for all his ancestors
the piece of land that he would hold until he died, under
quarantine. He didn't ask to be let out; he knew we wouldn't
let him, and so he died, king of his shrunken domain,
and after that, we went in, forgetfully, purposefully

insistent on forgetting, determined to make no new history;
to remember as little as possible. We have destroyed
the archives, we have shredded and wiped and erased
and burned. We have diaries in which we tear out the pages
as soon as we fill them, and on the shelves we store
nothing more than the empty book covers. We are visionary,
we believe, in our belief that there will be no more fighting,
as long as there is nothing to fight about.

The Last Black Hole

was not the last. The last black hole
was everything in the entire universe
collapsed into a space even smaller
than you can imagine. The last black
hole was the end of time, and then
it exploded into a new time, and then
there was a whole new universe,
the one we know, and what is coming
at the next black hole will be another
whole new universe, but not the one
we know. The one coming will be
a universe where nothing of us
will have survived, not even the tiniest speck,
except maybe the rediscovered
truth that there was a time in which we lived,
though this truth will be our truth,
not theirs, but you knew that,
didn't you, that every truth we have
is a human truth, that as long as
we're the ones looking, everything
will always look like us, and as sure
as every human will be born and die,
there is only our time, our journey
to the black hole and our journey
away from it, and don't be discouraged,
we do not give birth astride the grave
as some have said, but rather we are born
into a picture in which we are only a pixel,
and as the pigment shall never know

the painting, so we are fixed within our
place, and we must not fear because
we cannot see the design, and this
I call faith, knowing that the last black
hole is coming, and on the other side
will be time and space, and on the other side
will be time and space, and on the other
side will be time and space,
but without us.